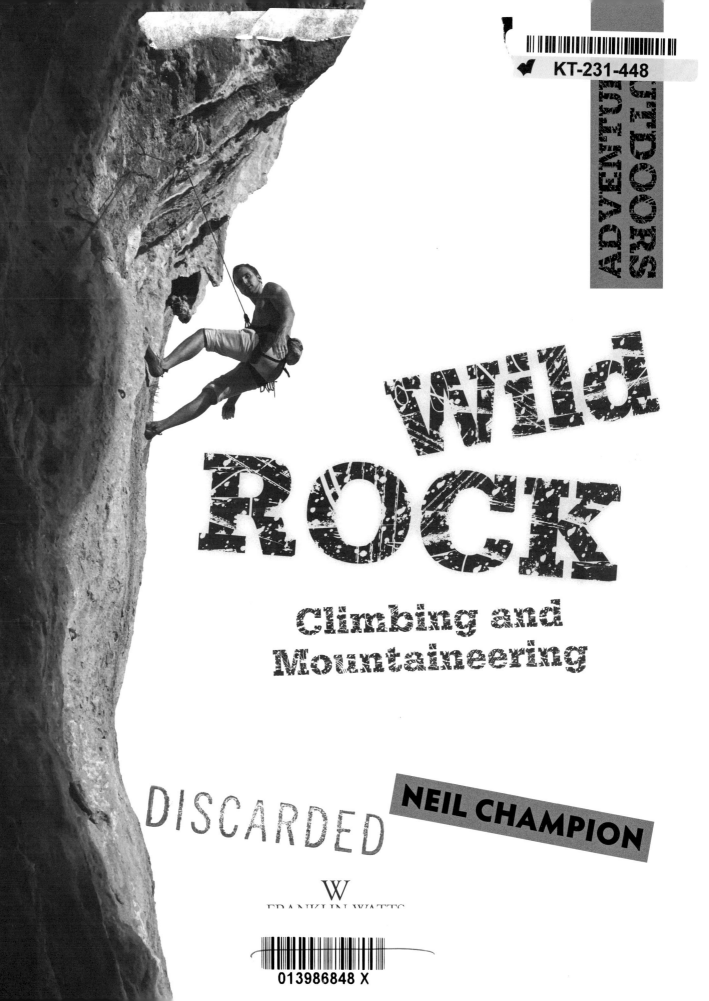

ADVENTURE OUTDOORS

Wild ROCK

Climbing and Mountaineering

NEIL CHAMPION

W
FRANKLIN WATTS

An Appleseed Editions book

Paperback edition 2014

First published in 2012 by Franklin Watts
338 Euston Road, London NW1 3BH

Franklin Watts Australia
Hachette Children's Books
Level 17/207 Kent St, Sydney, NSW 2000

© 2012 Appleseed Editions

Created by Appleseed Editions Ltd,
Well House, Friars Hill, Guestling,
East Sussex TN35 4ET

Designed and illustrated by Guy Callaby
Edited by Mary-Jane Wilkins
Photo research by Su Alexander

ISBN 978 1445 1 3170 2

Dewey Classification: 796.5 '223

All words in **bold** can be found in the Glossary on page 30.

A CIP catalogue for this book is available from
the British Library.

Picture credits
l = left, r = right, c = centre, t = top, b = bottom
Page 1 Andrey Bandurenko/Shutterstock; 2 Thinkstock; 4l Michael G
Smith/Shutterstock, r Swinner/Shutterstock; 5l Greg Epperson/
Shutterstock, r Stefan Petrovski/Shutterstock; 6tl Shcherbakov Ilya/
Shutterstock, tr Alysta/Shutterstock, b Marek Cech/Shutterstock;
7t Swinner/Shutterstock, b Daniel Prudek/Shutterstock; 8l Forbis/
Shutterstock, r Praseodimio/Shutterstock; 9 & 10 Thinkstock; 11t Eric
Bajart, bl Thinkstock, br Goodshot/Thinkstock;12t Michael Blann/
Thinkstock, c Thinkstock, b Jupiterimages/Thinkstock; 14 Main image
Shutterstock, tl Thinkstock, tr Greenland/Shutterstock, b Jan
Kranendonk/Shutterstock.com; 15t & bl Grafvision/Shutterstock,
br Michael Siegmund/Shutterstock; 16, 17 & 18 Thinkstock;
19 tl Jupiterimages/Thinkstock, cl Pierpaoloct, bl Hemera
Technologies/ Thinkstock, r Thinkstock; 20l Scottandwendi at en.
Wikipedia, r Thinkstock; 21l Stefa/Shutterstock, r Robnroll/
Shutterstock; 22 Thinkstock; 23t Trekandshoot/Shutterstock, b Iain
Lees; 24t Thinkstock, b Dim Dimich/Shutterstock; 25 Thinkstock;
26 Getty Images; 27 Thinkstock; 28 Aaron Twa/Shutterstock;
29t Thinkstock; 29l Robert Ranson/Shutterstock, cl Thinkstock, cr Joe
Gough/Shutterstock, r Thinkstock; 32t Worldinmyeyes.PL/Shutterstock,
b Roca/Shutterstock:

Front cover: Tyler Olson/Shutterstock

Printed in China

Franklin Watts is a division of Hachette Children's Books,
an Hachette UK company.
www.hachette.co.uk

Contents

Let's go climbing!

Our planet is a very rocky place. If you put all the mountains on Earth on top of each other, they'd reach beyond the moon. Why not explore them in one of the most exciting sports you can imagine – climbing.

People have been climbing for thousands of years, but only in the last 150 years have they begun to climb just for the challenge and adventure. Why do they do it?

Rising to a challenge

At first glance, climbing seems dangerous. Imagine being hundreds of metres up a sheer wall of rock a long way from safety. Your arms are aching and your legs are beginning to shake. How will you make it to the top?

This is where climbers rely on their training and skills, as well as team work. Most climbers

Two climbers tackle a sheer mountain face. The lower climber is anchored to the rock and is belaying the lead climber.

have a partner at the other end of the rope, and their limbs automatically remember how to find the next foothold. They need to keep calm and remember all the practice they've put in. That way they'll safely reach the point on the rock face they're aiming for.

Overcoming danger

Climbing and mountaineering appeal to our love of adventure and freedom, physical exercise and the triumph of overcoming danger by training to deal with risk. This is what climbing is about.

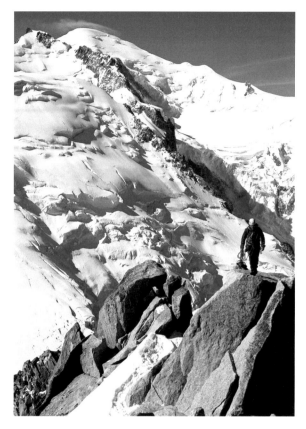

Left A partner and a thin rope stop this climber falling in Yosemite, USA.

Amazing FACTS

Most people climb in pairs, with each person tied to one end of the rope. One climber leads, while the other lets out rope. If the leader falls, their partner holding the other end of the rope (called the belayer) holds the rope firm to catch them. Only when the leader has reached the point they are aiming for does the belayer start to follow.

Getting started

You need skill to climb a rock face or scale a mountain – you can't simply have a go. New climbers need advice and training from people with years of experience.

Above *A young climber takes her first steps on a climbing wall.*

Left *Learning to tie on.*

You can join an outdoor club in your nearest town or at school, or join an organization such as the scouts or guides. Your local indoor climbing wall may have a club for young people.

TRUE Survivors

In January 2011 Adam Potter, a climber from Glasgow, survived an amazing 300-metre fall down a near vertical slope in Scotland almost unscathed. When mountain rescuers were sent to look for him they feared the worst. But when they found Adam, they were astonished to discover him standing up and looking at a map. This was despite the fact that he had slipped when trying to put on **crampons** and tumbled down three rocky crags to the valley floor. Experts say he was extremely lucky to survive, and even luckier to suffer only minor injuries.

Learning the ropes

All climbers start somewhere. Clubs can lend you equipment and teach you how to use it. Here are some of the knowledge and skills climbers need.

You need to know:

🪨 **How to use a map and a compass so you can navigate.**

🪨 **How to use equipment, such as a harness, helmet, ropes, belay devices, protection, and even axe and crampons for icy conditions.**

🪨 **How to tie knots, including the figure of eight, the clove hitch, the Italian hitch, and the overhand knot.**

🪨 **About climbing and mountaineering grades – these tell you how hard the climb will be.**

🪨 **Climbing calls, such as 'Climb when ready', 'Climbing', 'OK'.**

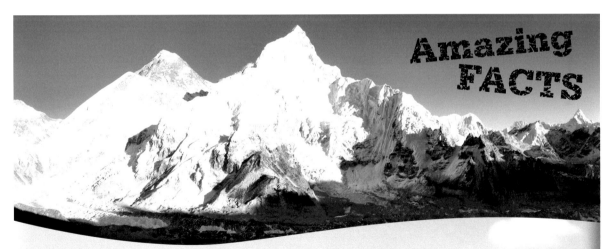

Amazing FACTS

Mount Everest is the highest mountain in the world, at 8,848m. It was formed when India collided with Asia millions of years ago. The mountain is part of the Himalaya, the highest mountain chain in the world.

Everest is still being pushed up a couple of centimetres a year, but it is not getting any higher. The top is being eroded (worn away) at a rate of about two centimetres a year, so it stays more or less the same height.

What type of kit?

Climbers need to learn to use climbing equipment, from special clothing and footwear to ropes, harnesses and helmets.

The right choice

All climbers need the right kit for the type of climbing they are doing. Rock boots and a chalk bag are all you need to climb indoors. Outside you need a harness, rope, protection, **slings** and **karabiners**, as well as a partner. Mountaineers need boots, warm waterproof clothing, a hat and gloves, a map, compass and rucksack.

Essential gear: hat and gloves, warm fleece and sunglasses to protect eyes from the sun's glare.

Modern climbers use rock boots, ropes and metal wedges called nuts as part of their climbing kit.

Amazing FACTS

A hundred years ago climbers tied a rope around their waists in case they fell. This kind of waist loop ends up around the climber's chest and could stop them breathing. Climbers today use a **sit harness**, which allows a climber who has fallen to sit in space, and prevents the waist belt riding up around the chest.

How modern ropes work

A modern climbing rope is strong enough to hold a two-tonne truck. The rope absorbs the energy of a fall by stretching, so prevents injuries. Imagine if a **bungee jumper** jumped off a bridge several hundred metres high attached to a metal cable. The cable would hold, but not stretch. The jumper would be injured or even killed. Jumpers use bungee cord because it works like an elastic band. It holds the climber and stretches to absorb the energy of the fall. This is what modern climbing ropes do.

core provides 80% of strength

tough outer layer or sheath

A bungee jumper flies through the air, protected by a strong, elastic cord tied to his legs.

USEFUL KNOTS

Bowline
Makes a loop at the end of a rope. Easy to untie.

Clove hitch
Attaches a rope to rock anchors or trees. Easy to untie.

Figure of eight
Attaches a climbing rope to a harness. Easy to untie.

Overhand
Stops the end of a rope unravelling. Hard to untie.

Choosing kit

Here are some top tips to help you get started. Take advice from experienced friends or teachers before buying or hiring kit.

Mountain boots

◉ **Must be comfortable and support the ankles.**

When buying boots, wear climbing socks. Walk up and down a slope in the shop. Badly fitting boots lift at the heel (causing blisters) and squash your toes when going downhill.

Harness

◉ **Should be padded and comfortable.**

Some harnesses have adjustable leg loops and waist belt as well as self-locking safety buckles. They are designed to support you if you are hanging on a rope. It's important to know what sort of harness you have.

Ropes

Should be suited to specific use. If in doubt ask an expert.

Rock shoes

- Allow you to feel footholds through the thin soles.

- Support your foot on small holds.

- Have sticky rubber soles.

Fit should be tight, but your toes should lie flat, touching the inside of your shoes.

TRUE Survivors

Edward Whymper was desperate to be the first to reach the summit of the Matterhorn. He had tried and failed eight times by 1865! Whymper started his ninth attempt in July 1865 with a team of seven, including an English lord and a vicar, as well as some Swiss climbing guides. This time they reached the top, just beating an Italian group. But that wasn't the end of the story. On the way down four climbers slipped and fell to their deaths. The others were saved because the rope connecting them to the four who fell snapped.

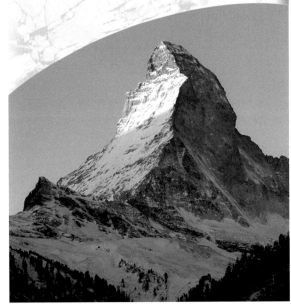

11

Climbing skills

Learn good techniques from the beginning. Climbers need to get up steep rock in a way that saves as much energy as possible. Fingers and arms tire first, so use your stronger feet and legs more. Good footwork, balance and efficient movement are more important than big muscles.

A young climber uses good footwork and balance on easy angled rock.

This climber has both hands on one long, thin hold. Climbers need strong fingers!

Centre of gravity

The **centre of gravity** for most people is around the belly button. When we climb, we shift our centre of gravity. This means we have to place one foot carefully on a hold and then put our weight over it so we can move the second foot. We can usually see holds for hands, so sometimes we put more weight on our arms than we need to.

Belaying

Belaying is a way of making sure that a climber who falls does not hit the ground. One end of a rope is fixed to a climber's harness. The rope then passes through fixed bolts or temporary fixings in the rock down to a person below, called the belayer. The belayer wears a harness with a belay device. The rope runs through the belay device and is controlled by the belayer, so that the climber above cannot fall and hit the ground.

Learning to belay

An expert or instructor can teach you how to belay. The pictures below show you how a belay device works for a right-handed climber.

belay device

karabiner

A *Thread the rope through a belay device and attach a karabiner to your harness.*

live rope attached to your climbing partner

dead rope falls to floor

karabiner clips through rope *and* belay device

your harness

karabiner locks securely

B *Take in the rope, following these five steps as your climbing partner goes up.*

live rope

dead rope

1 *With your left hand on the **live rope** and the right on the dead rope, keep the ropes parallel and take in the **dead rope**.*

2 *Bring the dead rope down towards your hip.*

3 *Move your left hand down from the live rope to the dead rope.*

4 *Move your right hand closer to the belay device.*

5 *Move your left hand back to the live rope and repeat the steps as the climber goes up.*

Climbing games

Footwork and balance are the keys to good climbing, rather than strong muscles.

When you are learning to climb, concentrate on where you place your feet to take the pressure off your arms and fingers. Small moves are better than high steps or strenuous pulls. Learn to be neat with your movement and climb like a cat. Try the games below at your local climbing wall to develop your technique.

Look at the body shapes of these climbers. Which look comfortable and balanced and which look as if they might be struggling?

Feet or hands?

Once you're on the climbing wall, move in any direction, hands first, then feet. Now start again, but this time lead with your feet and then move your hands. What do you notice? Most people feel less tired when they move feet first. This is because they push up off their feet rather than pulling up with their arms.

Body shapes

Climb on to the wall and find comfortable hand and foot holds. Keep your feet where they are and move your hands to any holds you can reach: high up, to the side or low down. What do you notice? Some of the body shapes you make will be very tiring. Now try moving just your

feet to as many different holds as you can. Body positions in which your centre of gravity is furthest from your feet are more difficult.

Turn into the wall

Climb to a vertical part of the climbing wall. Hang out from the wall with your arms straight, your feet on holds and your body in space. After a while your arms will tire. Pull yourself in, turning one hip to touch the wall. You should be able to stay in this position for longer because your weight is over your feet.

Amazing FACTS

The sport of slacklining started in Yosemite Valley in California, USA, in the 1970s. People walk along a climbing rope tied between two trees. The sport requires excellent balancing skills and strong muscles. Amazing feats of daring have since taken place in which a slackliner balances on a rope across a chasm hundreds of feet deep. One slip and you're gone...

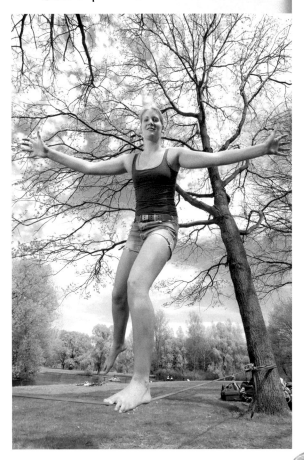

Top tips for training

Whether you are planning to climb a high mountain or a challenging area of overhanging indoor wall, you will need to do some training. This not only helps you climb harder and longer, it will also help you avoid injury.

Train for success

Plan your training around the goals you want to achieve. If you want to rock climb, train at your local climbing wall. If you aim to conquer mountains, you need to train on long walks with an increasingly heavy rucksack on your back.

Strength versus stamina

You can build up your strength by going **bouldering**. This involves short climbs without ropes over large boulders

Above *Carrying a large rucksack builds up leg muscles and stamina.*

Below *Short boulder climbs increase your strength and power.*

(which can be artificial). If you practise short hard moves at the climbing wall as hard as you can, this will strengthen your short twitch muscle fibres. **Endurance** exercises build up slow twitch muscle fibres. Make up some circuits at the climbing gym, choosing easy or moderately hard moves, but keep climbing for about 10-15 minutes.

Open and closed skills

To play any sport well, you need to practise some of the same movements over and over again – these are called closed skills. For example, serving in tennis. To climb well you also need open skills. These vary depending on where you are and what is happening around you. There are many ways to climb a particular route. Climbers need to train their muscles to find the best and most efficient way to approach any climb – not an easy task.

Amazing FACTS

Experiments have shown just how powerful our minds are when we exercise. Even thinking about physical training starts preparing your body for it. It does this by pumping chemicals into the bloodstream (for example, **adrenaline**) which help the muscles work extra hard. So you can prepare yourself for climbing by thinking about it beforehand.

Staying safe

There can be a fine line between having an adventure in the mountains and taking dangerous risks.

Good planning, the right equipment and companions, as well as choosing a sensible route all help to make sure you have fun and stay safe. But things can still go wrong even on a well planned trip, so it's good to know what to do in an emergency.

Climbers head into the mountains to tackle a route they have chosen – challenging but achievable.

TRUE Survivors

In July 1977, British climbers Doug Scott and Chris Bonington stood triumphantly on top of The Ogre. This 7,285-metre-high mountain in Pakistan is one of the hardest mountains in the world to climb. It is extremely steep and rocky, with no easy way to reach the summit.

As the climbers **abseiled** back down in the dark, Doug slipped on water ice, smashed into some rocks and broke both ankles. Then a storm blew in and the climbers were trapped high on the mountain for 24 hours. With the help of two other climbers, Doug eventually slid and crawled down to base camp.

To make matters worse, Chris smashed two ribs and became ill with **pneumonia** during the descent. It took them eight days in all, but the climbers survived thanks to the toughness and skills they had learned during their years of mountaineering.

Top ten survival tips

1 Learn to navigate in all conditions.

4 Know your limits: how skilled and fit you are. Climb within your limits.

5 Learn emergency calls. The distress signal in the mountains is 6 whistle blasts or 6 torch flashes in the dark. Wait one minute and start again. Rescuers give 3 blasts or flashes.

7 Learn how to make shelter for the night anywhere.

8 Learn how to find and purify water.

2 Learn to abseil (slide down a rope).

3 Learn to read the weather.

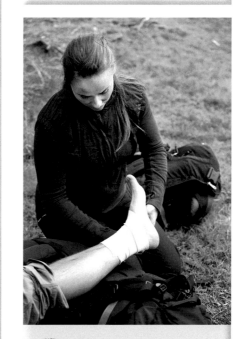

6 Learn first aid skills – they can save a life.

9 Take the right equipment and emergency food, but don't carry more than you need.

10 NEVER PANIC. In an emergency keep calm so you can decide what to do to get to safety.

Getting out of trouble

Climbing and mountaineering involve risk. You need to match your experience and fitness to the climb, so you can handle any dangers you meet. Then, even if something goes wrong, you can get yourself out of trouble.

TRUE Survivors

In 1992 mountaineer Colby Coombs was climbing Mount Foraker in Alaska with two friends. When a storm struck they decided to set off back down. Suddenly they were swept away by an **avalanche**. Coombs woke dangling from his rope, without pack or mittens.

He had broken his shoulder, ankle and bones in his neck. Both his friends were dead. He spent six days scrambling painfully down to safety. Today he teaches survival skills and says, '... if you get in trouble, anything that gets in the way of success has to be eliminated – emotion, fear, pain. It's the mental things that impede survival.'

Vertical caves, like the one above, and steep snow slopes are common hazards faced by mountain climbers.

Keep cool!

A cool head is essential when you're in trouble. If you become lost on a mountain, stay calm and try to work out where you are. Look at your map and find the last place you remember. What have you seen since leaving there? Piece together your route like a detective, then try to find the path you need on the map.

If you have to spend an unplanned night in the open, think of the important things you need to do to survive. Can you make a temporary home out of things around you – rock, wood, branches or snow? Do you have anything useful in your rucksack, such as a large polythene bag or sheet?

Anything that will keep out the cold night air is good. You can survive many days without food, but water is essential. Can you find any nearby? Can you purify it?

Winter mountaineering

When snow and ice cover the mountains you need to be able to use crampons and an ice axe. These help climbers grip the treacherous surface, when even standing up can be difficult. Navigation can be difficult in the snow, where everything can look the same and there's no **horizon** to focus on.

The right kit

In strong wind and freezing temperatures, the human body loses heat quickly without the right clothing. Apart from a windproof and waterproof **shell** (jacket and trousers), you need two fleece or wool layers, a thermal vest and **long johns**, warm trousers and wool socks. Several pairs of gloves, a hat and a scarf are also essential. For a firm footing you need crampons which fit your mountain boots as well as an axe.

Steep snow and ice demand special skills, clothing and equipment. This climber uses an ice axe and crampons to make progress.

TRUE Survivors

At around sunset on 24 September 1975 two men stood on the summit of Everest, the highest point on Earth. Doug Scott and Dougal Haston had just become the first British men to scale the south west face of the mountain. The temperature was about to drop to –40 degrees centigrade, but they did not have time to reach to their tent thousands of metres below them before dark. They had to try to survive the night over 8,500 metres up the mountain. They had no shelter, sleeping bags or stove. They did survive, but only because they knew how to dig a makeshift **snow hole**, which gave them some protection from the harsh wind and freezing night air. Without it they might have died, or lost toes and fingers to **frostbite**.

Digging for survival

You need to be able to dig a snow hole in an emergency to get out of the wind if you are to survive a night in a freezing landscape. Find a place where the snow is deep and has drifted – a hollow or the bank of a frozen stream. Use your ice axe to dig horizontally into the bank of snow. Your hole should be big enough for

Two mountaineers have fun digging a snow hole with two entrances.

you and your rucksack in a sitting position. Cut bricks of snow to block the entrance once you're inside, but make sure you leave a gap for air. Sit on your rucksack or climbing rope so you're not on the frozen ground.

Finding the way

Finding your way is a key skill. Guide books explain a route but you also need to work things out along the way.

Make sure you take all the safety kit you might need – map and compass, water and food, spare clothes and a torch.

Staying safe

Follow these rules when in the mountains:

ALWAYS LET PEOPLE KNOW WHERE YOU ARE GOING. FILL IN A ROUTE CARD.

DON'T TRAVEL ALONE.

KNOW THE ESCAPE ROUTES IF WEATHER TURNS BAD OR SOMEONE IS ILL.

DON'T BE AFRAID TO TURN BACK.

ALWAYS TAKE A MAP, COMPASS AND SPARE FOOD.

LEARN TO USE GPS, BUT REMEMBER, BATTERIES RUN OUT.

Check your map regularly when you are high in the mountains, so you always know where you are.

Maps and compass

A map and compass are powerful tools. Learn how to use them. The top of a map always points north and the **grid lines** go north-south and east-west. The moving arrow on a compass swings round to point to **magnetic** north-south. Most **contour** lines show a difference in height of ten metres. Blue indicates water – a river, lake or marsh. You can measure distances on your map using the ruler on the side, but you need to know the **scale** of the map.

Route-finding

A climbing guide book will tell you how to find the start of a route, what grade it is, and how high the climb goes. It will also tell you how to get back down. But once you start climbing, you may not remember the detail. Experience helps you spot where the route goes.

TRUE Survivors

In 2009, teenager Scott Mason was out for a day hike in the White Mountains in New Hampshire, USA. His aim was to climb Mount Washington. However, he got lost and spent three nights out in the open. He survived to tell his tale because he was an Eagle Scout who knew how to make emergency shelter and handle the hostile conditions. He was well equipped with warm clothing and an ice axe and crampons to cope with the snow.

Scrambling

Scrambling is a popular sport that mixes the adrenaline-rush of rock climbing with the satisfaction of getting to the top of a mountain.

As well as an easy trekking path, many rock hills and mountains have more difficult routes to the top. They may not be as hard as a true rock climb, but still require you to use your hands as well as your feet to stay safe. Some of the hard scrambles need a rope for safety on particularly tricky and exposed parts.

A head for heights

Scrambling can be dangerous because many scrambles take place on easy rock but have long drops below. You need a steady head. Make sure you learn to scramble with experienced people.

TRUE Survivors

In 2003 Aron Ralston was scrambling alone in Bluejohn Canyon in Utah's Canyonland National Park. A large boulder fell on his arm and trapped him. For nearly four days he tried to move it without success. When he ran out of water, he knew he would die unless he did something drastic. He cut off the trapped part of his arm with a penknife and eventually got to a place where he was spotted and rescued. Aron's story is now well known around the world since he wrote a book about his experiences, which was filmed as *127 Hours*.

Three points of contact

Always try to keep both hands and one foot or both feet and one hand on any rock you are scrambling up, especially if the rock is wet or slippery. Then if a hand or foot slips off, you have two other points of contact to help you regain your balance and avoid falling. Remember to keep your weight over your feet and use your legs as much as possible to push up rather than pull too heavily with your hands.

27

What do you know about climbing?

Are you ready to go climbing? Do you know what equipment you need, what to do if you get lost, or how to tie a clove hitch? Try this quiz and find out what you know about climbing and mountaineering. Answers on page 31.

▼ **1** Can you match knots with their names?
a Figure of eight
b Clove hitch
c Overhand knot
d Bowline

2 Which of these is a great place to learn how to climb?
a A forest
b A high mountain
c An indoor climbing wall
d A sports gym

3 Which of these is true?
a Ropes stretch to absorb the energy of a falling climber.
b The belayer always climbs first.
c A sit harness means you should not stand up wearing it.
d The map is the most important navigation tool you can buy.

4 What does bouldering mean?
a Looking after your climbing partner by holding the rope.
b Climbing at a low level indoors or outside without a rope or special gear and using a crash mat to fall.
c Running down a hillside leaping from rock to rock.
d Making piles of rock on a mountain trail to help find your way back.

7 You should take crampons when you might come across:
a Wild animals
b Other mountaineers
c Thick mist and fog
d Snow and ice

5 Shell clothing is called this because:
a It is made from the shells of small sea creatures.
b It is the outer clothing a mountaineer uses to keep wind and rain out.
c It is sponsored by a well known oil company.
d It is used only by the inhabitants of the Shell Islands.

8 Are these statements true or false?
a Dead rope means that the rope is old and you should throw it away.
b A snow hole is an emergency shelter that can be dug quickly to get out of icy conditions in the winter mountains.
c It doesn't really matter if you can navigate in the mountains, as it is not very important.
d Balance and good footwork are key to good climbing technique.

▼ 6 Link the climbing equipment to the names.
a rucksack **b** harness
c sling **d** karabiner

1

2

3

4

29

Glossary

abseil To slide down a rope in a controlled way.

adrenaline A chemical our bodies make to help us run from danger or fight it.

avalanche Snow that breaks away from a slope and moves fast downhill.

belay device A piece of climbing equipment that attaches to a rope and halts a falling climber.

bouldering Climbing at a low level without ropes, harness or a belay device.

bungee jump A jump off a high place attached to a bungee cord.

centre of gravity A point by the belly button that marks where the part of the body above weighs about the same as the part below.

contour A line on a map that shows equal height above sea level.

crampons Metal spikes that attach to mountain boots. They dig into snow and ice to stop climbers slipping.

dead rope The part of a rope that comes from the belay device that is used as a brake when locked off to halt a falling climber.

endurance The aspect of fitness training that allows people to go on working hard for a long time. In running, a marathon is the ultimate endurance test.

frostbite Damage done usually to fingers and toes by extreme cold.

grade The level of difficulty of a specific climb, at an indoor wall or outside on a crag or mountain cliff.

grid lines Straight lines on a map that run north-south and east-west.

horizon The point where the sky meets the ground.

karabiner A metal ring used to join two things together, such as a rope and a harness.

live rope The part of the rope that comes from the belay device and goes to the climber.

long johns A warm inner layer worn under trousers.

magnetic Relating to magnetic north, a place near the North Pole where compasses point to.

navigate Being able to use a map, compass and natural signs to find the way around an area.

pneumonia A serious infection of the lungs.

purify To remove chemicals or bacteria from water so it is safe to drink.

route card A form climbers fill showing their route in case they get lost.

scale The scale of something is the relationship between its size on a map and its real size.

shell Waterproof and windproof outer clothing which protects against bad weather.

sit harness A harness with leg loops attached to a belt, which keeps a falling climber in a sitting position in mid-air.

sling Strong, light supporting climbing equipment.

snow hole A shelter dug into a deep bank of snow. It can be small enough for one person or big enough to sleep ten!

Websites

www.kidsclimbing.co.uk UK Kids Climbing

www.thebmc.co.uk British Mountaineering Council

www.usaclimbing.net USA Climbing

www.mountaineering.ie Mountaineering Council of Ireland

www.mcofs.org.uk Mountaineering Council of Scotland

www.climbing.com.au Climbing Australia

www.mojozone.co.nz Climb New Zealand

Books

Get Outdoors: Rock Climbing Neil Champion, Wayland, 2008

Rock Climbing Tim Seeberg, Child's World, 2004

Extreme Sports: Rock Climbing John E Schindler, Gareth Stevens Publishing, 2005

Rock Climbing Libby Peter, Mountain Leader Training UK, 2004

Indoor Climbing Pete Hill, Cicerone, 2009

Quiz answers

1

b. clove hitch   *c. overhand*

d. bowline   *a. figure of eight*

2 *c*

3 *a and d are true*

4 *b*

5 *b*

6

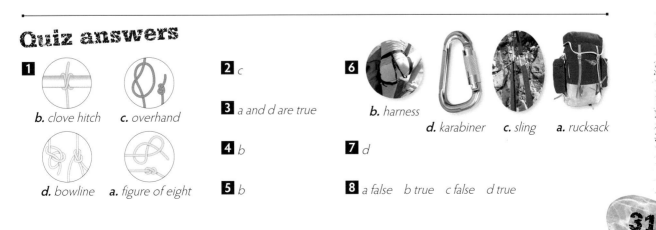

b. harness

d. karabiner   *c. sling*   *a. rucksack*

7 *d*

8 *a false   b true   c false   d true*

Index